to my parent,

by freya winters

this book is for:

_____

introduction:

this book is a labor of love, dedicated to
you—my cherished parent. within these pages,
you'll find 100 days' worth of loving reminders,
gentle encouragements, and heartfelt words
of appreciation. crafted to be a daily source of
inspiration, my hope is that these words lift up your
heart and soothe your soul.

while words may never fully capture the depth
of my love for you, i trust that they can provide
a glimpse into the profound appreciation and
affection i hold in my heart.

with all my love,

....

DAY 1

before delving into the pages of this book, i want you to know that i am *forever* grateful for the gift of life you've given me. without you, i wouldn't have experienced this world, and without you, i wouldn't have known what unconditional love is. i truly adore you, and i hope that each day you read these pages, you are reminded of that.

DAY 2

i want to thank you for listening to me.
not only that, but for *hearing* me.
for trying to gain further understanding and
insight of my words,
for acknowledging my mind and emotions,
and for ensuring i feel safe and seen.

DAY 3

if you were ever in doubt and i wasn't there to
reassure you, i want you to know that i couldn't
have asked for a better parent—and i truly
mean that,

from the bottom of my heart.

DAY 4

the happiness you bring to those around you speaks
volumes about who you are.

please keep on illuminating the world with your light.

DAY 5

please never forget:

you're not too sensitive,
you're not too loud,
you're not too much,
you're not too emotional,
you're not a burden,
you're not difficult to be around,
you're not lazy for needing to rest,
you're not destined for failure,
you're not weak,
you're not failing.

you're doing an astounding job at life
keep doing your thing;

you're making a much more positive impact on the world
around you than you realize.

DAY 6

START GIVING YOURSELF THE LOVE YOU GIVE
SO FREELY TO EVERYONE ELSE. (i insist!)

DAY 7

i love you deeply, more than words can express.
it's a profound and overwhelming love that resides in
my heart for you. unfortunately, words can't
fully capture it.

it's a love that goes beyond this world—a truly
beautiful connection we share.

DAY 8

i hope you know, no matter how far i go or
where i travel, you will always be my home and
one of the only places i truly feel safe.

DAY 9

your strength inspires me every waking moment.
the trials and tribulations you've experienced to ensure i
had a good shot at life will never go unnoticed.

i see you.
i hear you.
i appreciate you *endlessly*.

DAY 10

if you're reading this with worries on your mind and a
heaviness in your heart, remember that these feelings will
pass. you *will* feel better, notice the beauty that lies within
this world, and wake up with the weight of the world
lifted off your shoulders. your negative thoughts and
emotions are temporary;

better days are coming.

DAY 11

thank you for this beautiful heart.
thank you for my incredible life.
thank you for pushing me out of my comfort zone.
thank you for allowing me the space to make mistakes and grow.
thank you for holding my hand and telling me everything is
gonna be ok.
thank you for loving every part of me when i made it really
difficult to do so.
thank you for bringing so much good energy into my life.
thank you for *everything*.

DAY 12

having you as my parent helped me fall in love with life.
i'm thrilled to explore more of what this planet has to
offer, and the best part?

you're here to experience it with me.

DAY 13

simply put,

without you, i wouldn't be the person i am today. your love
has guided me toward becoming the best possible version of
myself—a version inspired by the deepest depths of your heart.
thank you for being my guiding light, my biggest inspiration,
and my *hero.*

DAY 14

i don't know if i've ever told you this or not, but i want you to know that it's okay if you feel you didn't always get everything right. yes - you are my parent, but you are still human, too.

you did an incredible job;
please don't ever doubt that, not for one second.

DAY 15

i'm not sure if you've forgotten, but their burdens are not yours to carry. their drama is not your responsibility. their regrets have nothing to do with you. their mistakes are their own. stop trying to fix everyone.

to my parent - freya winters

DAY 16

thank you for showing me it's brave to try. that
being different and standing up for what's right
isn't wrong. that adventure is important, and
exploration is life-changing.

that love exists everywhere, and that i'm worthy of
every last bit of it.

DAY 17

send this message to your inner child today:

you were never too much. you were always enough. there is and always was enough space for you in this world. none of what happened to you was ever your fault.

you're safe now.
everything is okay.

DAY 18

i hope you're proud of yourself for getting through those impossible days. take a moment to appreciate yourself and the work you've done for yourself and for your family.

i hope you can look back on your life and be content with what you've achieved, and i hope you can learn to love yourself just as you've loved us.

to my parent - freya winters

DAY 19

you've made my existence easier, lighter, and filled
with so many laughs. thank you for the pleasure of
being alive.

DAY 20

you're a stellar example of a human being.
an absolute beauty of a soul.
a haven amidst a storm.
my safe place.

DAY 21

the love you've shared will undoubtedly return to you
in the most beautiful ways.

keep an eye out for it; there's so much more to come.

DAY 22

repeat after me:

i am at peace with my past.
i am in love with my present,
and i am excited for whatever the future brings.

DAY 23

i love that i've been able to embrace every single version of you over the years. while you've grown and evolved, you've consistently remained true to yourself. you've always been the person your children have needed you to be—an incredible source of inspiration.

DAY 24

if there's anything i want the most for you - it's for you to fall head over heels in love with being *alive*.

DAY 25

not only are you my parent, but you're one of my
best friends, and i feel like one of the luckiest
people alive to be able to say that.

DAY 26

thank you for allowing me to be my true self all of these years. growing up wasn't always easy, as i'm sure you can understand. but growing up with you as my parent allowed me to express myself in ways that led me to be the person i am today.

DAY 27

how your life feels is *infinitely* more important than how it looks. it will do you the world of good to refrain from comparing yourself to other people's highlight reels. what you see on social media is rarely ever real life. focus on you, and focus on creating a beautiful life for yourself, and watch everything else fall into place.

to my parent - freya winters

DAY 28

you really are important to me.
you always have been,
and you *always* will be.

DAY 29

growing up taught me that we're all navigating life for the first time, including you. i'm sorry if i haven't always been as patient and understanding as you've needed me to be.
i hope you can forgive me.

to my parent - freya winters

DAY 30

i really feel the extended time that we spend apart.
it's just not the same until we're back together again.

DAY 31

how grateful i am that you taught me how to communicate with the people around me. not just to talk, but to listen, and to *understand.*

thank you for empowering me.

DAY 32

it would break my heart to think you ever feel guilty about any shortcomings you may think you've had. our journey, with its ups and downs, has been instrumental in shaping me into the person i am today, and i wouldn't have it any other way. your resilience and love during those challenging moments taught me valuable lessons about strength and compassion, and this shared experience has created a bond that's uniquely ours—a bond i cherish deeply.

DAY 33

you're loved.
you're appreciated.
you're adored.
you're looked up to.
you're our inspiration.
you're powerful.
you're worthy of amazing things.
you're a beautiful human,
with an even more beautiful soul.
you've come such a long way,
and you deserve *eternal* happiness.

DAY 34

having me enter the world as your child must have
been such a heavy adjustment for you, and i'm in awe
of how you managed to balance everything on your
shoulders in such a perfect way.

DAY 35

if you're the blueprint for my life,
then i know i'm doing pretty darn good.

DAY 36

i want you to understand that your love, patience, and empathy were never in vain. even if it may have seemed that way at times, i assure you it wasn't. they turned out to be the essential building blocks of the person i'm proud to say i'm becoming. every small sacrifice and glimmer of kindness contributed to the foundation of who i am. you did an outstanding job, and it's crucial to me that you *never* forget that.

DAY 37

your love is what taught me how to have empathy.
your love is what gave me the strength to make it
through the impossible days.
your love is the thing that inspires me every
waking moment to be better, to do better.
your love is what guides me to make the
right choices and stand with adversity.
your love is everything i've ever needed,

and *so* much more.

DAY 38

if a genie granted me one wish in this life, it would be to have you by my side until i leave this earth.

your presence means everything to me, and you are the embodiment of all that i am and aspire to be.

DAY 39

have you ever considered that maybe you're feeling
tired because you're doing a lot, but not enough
of what truly makes your heart happy?

DAY 40

some powerful affirmations for the best parent that ever lived:

my inner world creates and shapes my outer world.

i have everything i need within me to create the
change i want to see.

i am in touch with my thoughts and emotions,
not against them.

my worth is never defined by my levels of productivity.

DAY 41

some little reminders:

it's never too late; crying is not and *never* will be an indication of weakness, and life becomes peaceful when you realize you can't control everything.

DAY 42

this is a message for when life starts to feel really heavy again:

stop being so hard on yourself. nothing flourishes when you force it. you wouldn't speak to me the way you speak to yourself, so why do it? you were a child once, and that childlike wonder and innocence are still within you. find it, nurture it, and be patient with yourself.

you'll never bully yourself into finding peace.

DAY 43

i love you. with my whole heart.
my soul. my everything.
i appreciate you more than i'll ever
be able to portray with words.

to my parent - freya winters

DAY 44

thank you for hearing me when my voice has fallen upon deaf ears.

DAY 45

you've done an incredible job at life. i hope you take
some time to be proud of yourself and everything
you've achieved.

DAY 46

you're a absolute dream of a parent—take my word for it. i
am a living testament to your exceptional parenting.
if i could review my experience with you as my parent,
i'd need 6 stars and an 80,000-word allowance to even
come close to touching on how profoundly positive your
impact has been on me.

DAY 47

no amount of worrying will ever change an outcome for the better. take a deep breath. release whatever it is that's on your mind. repeat after me: "everything is happening as it should." take another deep breath. i'm proud of you. i'm rooting for you.

i believe in you.

to my parent - freya winters

DAY 48

you've spent year, after year, after year, putting everyone else before yourself. *it's your turn now.* on the day that you're reading this page, promise me this: you'll do one thing today to put a smile on your face. (and tell me when you've done it!)

DAY 49

i don't know if i've mentioned this lately, but i'm *always* here for you, just as you've been here for me. i want to hear about your day, and the challenges you're facing. i want to offer you a comforting hug and assure you that everything will be okay. i've got your back. i care about you endlessly and wish for nothing more than to see you as the happiest person to walk this earth.

DAY 50

the thing about you is that you can always sense when someone is a good fit for me or not—be it friends, partners, or strangers, you just know. it's a superhuman ability you possess. over the years, i've grown to trust your judgment increasingly because i'm aware that you always have my best interests at heart, and you can see through façades.

DAY 51

i want to thank you for loving and caring for me
on the hardest days you've had to experience. you're
a shining example of a parent, and i'm beyond
honored to be connected to you.

DAY 52

i promised myself never to take your love for granted, to always be present when we're together, to share a laugh at your (seriously) un-funny jokes, and most importantly, to appreciate you for everything you've done for me.

DAY 53

you're enough, even on the days of self-doubt.
you're enough, even on the mornings when getting out
of bed is a struggle.
you're enough, even when your demons tempt you to
hide away from the world.
you're enough, *always*.

DAY 54

thanks for never giving up on me, for having faith that
i would achieve greatness. thanks for loving me even
when i've pushed you away, for being the one constant
in my life, for trusting my dreams.

i love you more than you'll ever know.

DAY 55

the bond we have is different.
it's unique. it's special.
together, we navigate the world, growing, healing, and
progressing. reaching milestones side by side, and we discover
something new about ourselves every single day.

our souls were meant to explore this world side by side.

to my parent - freya winters

DAY 60

your support has propelled me to higher places.
your strength has driven me to do better.
your grace has made me move with patience.
your heart has shown me what unconditional love truly is.

DAY 61

as i've grown up, i now realize there have been many times (way too many) when i made it difficult for you to be the parent you wanted to be. i'm sorry for all the times i tested you and your patience. your grace throughout my periods of growth has been unmatched.

DAY 62

considering the circumstances that have shaped our lives, you have an incredible amount to be proud of. not only have you consistently and wholeheartedly shared your love, but you've also inspired me to do the same for those around me. your love will keep expanding around you and beyond.

your love is a *movement*.

DAY 63

please do me a favor, and go easy on yourself. don't beat
yourself up for your mistakes and misjudgements, but
practice patience and understanding, just as you have
for your children. you deserve the standard of love that
you share with others, and then some.

DAY 64

of all the things you've done for me over the years, the one that's always resonated the most has been the way you make me feel. the way you reassure me and take my worries away with your hugs, and the relief i feel when you hold my hand and tell me everything is going to be ok. you make me feel at home no matter where we are.

DAY 65

i'll always be grateful for the relationship we have. not only do we have a beautiful bond, but we can laugh until it hurts. i absolutely love laughing with you. our boundaries are healthy, and our intentions always pure. you're so incredibly important to me. please don't ever forget that.

DAY 66

in case you've forgotten, you're allowed to rest. you don't need to fill up every moment of time. effective self-care involves taking a moment, or two (or three!), and allowing some space to breathe.

remember, rest *is* productive.

DAY 67

i just want to remind you that whatever you're holding off from, *it's not too late.* you can start from a place of weakness and still surpass your own expectations.

DAY 68

you kept going,

and that really is something to be proud of.

DAY 69

i can't stress enough how important and impactful it has been to witness you break the cycle of challenges passed through our family and move forward in the way you know best—with love. your actions are already shifting things in a positive direction. thank you for focusing on healing rather than deepening the wounds.

DAY 70

because of you,

i am passionate.
i am sensitive.
i am brave.
i am strong.
i am empathetic,
and i am kind.

because of you
i choose action over stagnancy,
honesty over lies,
and courage over cowardice.

because of you,
life is beautiful,
and i know that everything is going to be okay.

DAY 71

not only did you bring me into this world, you showed me
how to live it with purpose, intention, and gratitude. you gave
me life, and then you gave me *life*.

it's absolute magic.

DAY 72

some affirmations for my parent:

whatever i am able to achieve today is more than enough.

i choose to feel at home within my body.

i believe in myself to my core.

i am inherently powerful.

DAY 73

i know it's been difficult to let me go over the years—to let me venture out into the big wide world and allow me to make my own mistakes. thank you for understanding my need to see what's out there, and thank you for giving me the freedom to do so.

but please don't worry; i'll always come back to you.

to my parent - freya winters

DAY 74

not only am i lucky enough to call you my parent, but also my best friend. i trust you with the entirety of my heart, and i know that, no matter what, you're there to hold my hand and guide me through the hardest parts of life.

to my parent - freya winters

DAY 75

our connection is one to be admired. our
souls are at ease with each other, and i don't
know how else to describe it—we just *click*.

DAY 76

your strength empowers me to hold my head high,
your love is the reason i believe that i'm allowed to take up space.
your soul brings forth my inner smile,
and your heart propels me forward with grace.

DAY 77

i don't think you have any idea of the happiness that i feel when i see you smile. your contentment is incredibly important to me, much more than you realize.

DAY 78

the fact you've allowed me to grow and flourish
without trying to mold me into someone you wanted
me to be is something i'll be forever grateful for.

DAY 79

i want to apologize for the times i've snapped at you and dismissed your love. you always deserved kindness.

DAY 80

your worth is not defined by your level of productivity.

read that again.

DAY 81

repeat after me:

better things are coming.
i am worthy of peace.
i am worthy of happiness.
i deserve to feel unconditional love, from others,
but more importantly myself.
i'm worthy of living a beautiful life.

DAY 82

stop waiting for everything to be perfect before you allow yourself to enjoy life. set a boundary with yourself now and make the decision to stop postponing happiness. you're way too important to let life pass you by.

DAY 83

having you as my parent meant that

i learned to cherish the little things
i had someone who believed in me from the very beginning
& it meant that i had the best possible start in life.

DAY 84

my grandma always told me "keep the people who feel like sunlight close to your heart". so please don't go anywhere.

you're my sunshine.

DAY 85

i know i'm older now, and we don't spend as much time together anymore, but please know that you are irreplaceable, and i will always need you and the love you give,

no matter where we are in the world.

to my parent - freya winters

DAY 86

despite all the darkness around you,
you always managed to find the light within yourself.

DAY 87

i've always cherished the smaller things you've done for me, from tidying my messy teenage bedroom to sitting with me in silence when i've just needed your company.

to my parent - freya winters

DAY 88

fyi;

you're honestly the best parent anyone could've ever asked for.

to my parent - freya winters

DAY 89

it's not your job to be everything to everyone.

DAY 90

here's your reminder to take that risk and pursue that thing
you've been postponing. the one you know will bring you
joy and elevate you to the next level. you've given me the
strength to do the same growing up, and now it's time to
take some of your own advice. don't let things become
stagnant. you're strong enough for whatever you're aiming
to achieve. you're capable.

you're brave.
you've got me right here,
and i'm not going anywhere.

DAY 91

this is your reminder that it's never the right decision
to hide away if you're struggling. you're not a burden,
you never were, and you never will be. let me help
you if i can. i want nothing more than for you to have
a peaceful mind. we've got this.

let's help each other *flourish.*

to my parent - freya winters

DAY 92

i need you to know that you can trust me
wholeheartedly, no matter what. our trust is built
on the firm foundations you've created for us.
you can lean on me whenever you need.

DAY 93

some (more) powerful affirmations for
the best parent that ever lived:

i deserve to rest, to recuperate, and to heal.

i am lucky. i am abundant. i am a winner.

the silent battles i'm fighting will pass.

i am so much more powerful than i give myself credit for.

i am allowed to love the person i am, the person i was, the person
i'm growing to become.

to my parent - freya winters

DAY 94

a little reminder:

stop trying to fix people. that's not your job.

DAY 95

i want you to begin selecting more activities that bring you peace, that make your heart happy, and that help you forget about the sadness in the world. it's time to shift some focus onto yourself.

it's time to prioritize your own happiness.

DAY 96

even on my darkest days, your light and energy provide the strength to persevere. you instil in me hope, faith, and drive. thank you for giving me life.

DAY 97

another day being loved by you truly is a dream come true.

to my parent - freya winters

DAY 98

the countless times you prioritized your family's happiness
over your own haven't gone unnoticed.

DAY 99

i hope you never have to shrink yourself to fit someone's ideal. it's not your responsibility to cater to anyone else's comfort.

to my parent - freya winters

DAY 100

i'm going to make you *so* proud.

Made in United States
Orlando, FL
26 September 2024